A BEACON BIOGRAPHY

TOM HOLLAND

Nicole K. Orr

PURPLE TOAD
PUBLISHING

Printing   1   2   3   4   5   6   7   8   9

A Beacon Biography

Angelina Jolie
Anthony Davis
Big Time Rush
Cam Newton
Carly Rae Jepsen
Carson Wentz
Daisy Ridley
Drake
Ed Sheeran
Ellen DeGeneres
Elon Musk
Ezekiel Elliott
Harry Styles of One Direction
Jennifer Lawrence

John Boyega
Kevin Durant
Lorde
Malala
Maria von Trapp
Markus "Notch" Persson, Creator of Minecraft
Misty Copeland
Mo'ne Davis
Muhammad Ali
Neil deGrasse Tyson
Peyton Manning
Robert Griffin III (RG3)
Tom Holland
Zendaya

Publisher's Cataloging-in-Publication Data
Orr, Nicole K.
    Tom Holland / written by Nicole K. Orr.
        p. cm.
Includes bibliographic references, glossary, and index.
ISBN 9781624693205
1. Motion picture actors and actresses—Great Britain--Biography—Juvenile literature. I. Series: Beacon biography.
    PN2598 2017
    791.4

Library of Congress Control Number: 2017940575

eBook ISBN: 9781624693090

ABOUT THE AUTHOR: Nicole K. Orr has been writing for as long as she has known how to hold a pen. She is the author of several other books for young readers and has won National Novel Writing Month ten times. Orr lives in Portland, Oregon, and camps under the stars whenever she can. She also likes traveling the world and taking road trips.

PUBLISHER'S NOTE: This story has not been authorized or endorsed by Tom Holland.

CONTENTS

Losing,
Then Winning

Tom Holland was sitting in his bedroom at his computer. His dog, Tessa, was sleeping on his bed. He had just gotten back from playing golf with his dad. It hadn't been a good week for Tom. Not only had he lost the golf game, but he had still not heard from Marvel on whether he was going to be their new Spider-Man. He had been waiting for months.

Looking online at Instagram, he spotted an announcement from Marvel. They *had* chosen the new Spider-Man. Holland sighed. Since no one had called him, he figured Marvel had chosen someone else for the role.

He clicked on the news release to see who the lucky actor was. Holland saw his name jump onto the screen! He slapped his laptop shut. He leaped to his feet. He began shouting with excitement at Tessa. He flew downstairs to where his family was.

"Guys! Guys! Guys! Guys! I'm going to be Spider-Man! I'm going to be Spider-Man!" Holland spoke so fast, it was almost impossible to understand him.

When Holland played Spider-Man, he used more than 20 different Spider-Man suits. Each had a certain purpose, such as the stunt suit or the camera-ready suit.

Kevin Feige is the mastermind behind Marvel Studios. He mines memorable stories from the golden era of Marvel Comics and brings them to the screen. He believes that the films should always remain faithful to the original material.

Tom's brother Harry was sitting on the couch. He shook his head and said that Marvel had likely been hacked. The announcement couldn't be true. If Marvel had chosen Tom for their new Spider-Man, they would have called him.

Tom finally called Marvel to find out what was happening, but no one seemed to know there, either. It took a phone call from the president of Marvel Studios, Kevin Feige, to get the truth.

"We want to cast you as the new Spider-Man," Feige told Tom.

"I know, Kevin! You put it on Instagram. I saw it!" Tom replied.

Within the next hour, the entire world would know it, too.[1]

Tom Holland is just one of many Marvel stars who were born in London. This includes Tom Hiddleston (Thor's villainous brother Loki), Benedict Cumberbatch (Doctor Strange), and Charlie Cox (Daredevil).

A Family of Stars

Thomas Stanley "Tom" Holland was born on June 1, 1996 in London, England. Even as a kid, Tom had a little bit of spider in him. His hobbies weren't spinning spider webs to swing from buildings, but he did love jumping on the huge trampoline in his backyard. He also loved free running, moving very quickly, and jumping over large objects. Tom would do flips, rolls, lunges, and jumps for hours. He'd come home bruised but smiling.

From the very beginning, Tom already had a really big fan: his father. Dominic Holland was a successful comedian and author. He thought his son was amazing, and he wanted the whole world to know it. Dominic created a blog called *Eclipsed*. The blog was about how fast the son was becoming a bigger star than the father. People thought it was so funny, Dominic turned it into an eBook called *How Tom Holland Eclipsed His Dad*.

Tom's mother, Nicola Elizabeth, was a photographer. She, too, played a very big role in her son's life. As he told *Teen Vogue*, "I completely and utterly rely on my mum. Without my mum, I would not be anywhere at all. I'd literally just be a couch potato."[1]

Are Holland's brothers jealous that he's famous? Not when they got to spend five months learning to surf in Thailand while Holland was filming a movie!

Tom has three brothers. Sam, Harry, and Patrick (Paddy) have never been jealous of their older brother. In fact, they like to be in front of the camera, too. YouTube has several videos of the Holland brothers playing pranks on one another.

Tom went to Donhead Preparatory School and to Wimbledon College (a high school). He danced for the first time at the BRIT School for Performing Arts and Technology. This school is for kids fourteen to nineteen years old who want to learn about all aspects of performance and art. It is the same school that the singers Adele and Amy Winehouse attended.

Tom also joined the Nifty Feet Dance School. That was when the magic happened! The dance school was performing at the Richmond (England) Dance Festival. Tom was on stage. Someone very important was watching him: casting director Lynne Page. Page was about to change Tom's life.

While attending Wimbledon College (above), Holland performed in Billy Elliot: The Musical *for the very first time.*

Holland was London's 17th boy to play Billy Elliot in **Billy Elliot: The Musical.**

From Wet to Hot to Cold

Tom Holland's first job was for something he didn't know how to do very well: dance. After Lynne Page watched him at the Richmond Dance Festival, she invited him to audition for *Billy Elliot: The Musical*. The story is about a boy who is training to be a boxer but dreams of dancing ballet.

Holland was nothing like the other boys at the audition. He didn't have any of the serious training they had. The casting team took one look at Holland and agreed that he didn't know how to dance. Page told them that they needed to teach him.

Eight auditions and two years of training later, Holland was cast as Michael, the best friend of Billy Elliot. A few months later, he was playing Billy Elliot himself.

Nobody would ever say again that Holland couldn't dance. For nearly two years, he played Billy Elliot, performing in 180 shows. To celebrate the fifth anniversary of the musical, he and three other boys who played the same role were invited to meet Gordon Brown, the Prime Minister of the United Kingdom. In May 2010, Holland did his last performance and went back home to his family in London. He wasn't home for very long.

Holland played Shô in the British film version of Studio Ghibli's *Arrietty*. (In the United States, the film is called *The Secret World of Arrietty*.) It was his first time being a voice actor in an animated film. What was the hardest

part of playing Shô? Holland said it was matching his words to the way the character's mouth moved.

In 2011, Holland was cast in a movie called *The Impossible*. When he came to the audition, he didn't know what the movie was actually about. "I knew my character's mum was in danger and the director asked me to write a letter to her and recite it," Holland said in an interview with *The Evening Standard*. "I started crying because it was genuinely sad, and I could see him welling up, too."[1]

The Impossible was physically demanding, but in a different way from *Billy Elliot: The Musical*. *The Impossible* was about a tsunami hitting the hotel where a family was staying. Holland played Lucas, the son of the two main characters.

When Holland played Shô in Arrietty, he was never actually face-to-face with the other actors. He recorded his lines in a recording booth while the voices of the other actors played through speakers around him.

The Impossible *was based on a real tsunami in Thailand. When Holland starred in the film, he met the family that inspired the movie.*

"I was being thrown around on wires, being dragged underwater and all that sort of stuff," he said to *SheKnows* about the experience. "And I loved it."[2]

For his role in *The Impossible*, Holland received the Hollywood Spotlight Award. At the National Board of Review, he received an award in the Breakthrough Actor category. At the Nevada Critics Awards, he also won Best Youth Performance.

In 2013, Holland was in a movie called *Locke*. The main character, Locke, spends the movie making 36 phone calls from his car. Locke's son Eddie, played by Holland, is never actually seen onscreen. Viewers only hear his voice, yet Holland left a strong impression on them.

Next, Holland took a role in *How I Live Now*. This movie follows the effects that a bombing had on a broken family. Holland plays Isaac, one of the sons. It was a very emotional role, but that part was easy for Holland.

Meg Rosoff wrote the novel on which the movie is based. She told *Film4*, "I remember Tom telling me that he was supposed to cry and be really, really upset during the scene in which the kids are separated, and he said he didn't have to act it at all. He was so upset when filming that scene that he was just crying, and that's because they'd bonded so much and become such good friends."[3]

From movies, Tom was cast in his first television show, *Wolf Hall*. In a world of kings and crowns, Holland plays Gregory Cromwell, the son of the main character. Holland's father always made sure to tune in for his son's episodes. He would often post on Twitter to get other people to watch the show, too.

Next, Holland directed and appeared in *Tweet*, a family-based video less than five minutes long. The short is about a grandfather who helps his grandson build a birdhouse. The video gave Holland's family the chance to shine along with him. Holland's brother Harry plays the grandson, and brothers Sam and Paddy also appear.

Holland has said that being in **Wolf Hall** *was the only film where he felt totally lost. He was lucky that costar* **Mark Rylance** *was there to give him advice.*

For *The Impossible*, Holland spent the first part of filming soaking wet. He didn't think it could get much worse—but he discovered it could when he was cast in the movie *In the Heart of the Sea*. The film is about a ship that is struck by a giant whale and slowly sinks into the ocean. (The true story on which the film is based inspired the novel *Moby Dick*.) During the shoot, Holland worked with Chris Hemsworth, the actor who plays Thor in the Avengers movies. When asked in an interview with *ComingSoon* if Holland could captain his own ship one day, Holland said, "With two oars maybe, but no sails."[4]

When Holland starred in *The Lost City of Z*, he found he missed being soaked. Why? Now he was stuck in the hot and humid Amazon rainforest. The movie is about an explorer and his son, played by Holland. Together, they search for a lost city called Z.

After Holland experienced the cold ocean and the steamy Amazon, it was time for another change. In *The Edge of Winter*, Holland plays one of several sons stranded in a cabin during a blizzard. With a snowstorm outside, the father tries to keep his boys alive.

By this time, Holland was still a teenager. He had already had some amazing experiences. He had worked with a few famous actors, and most of the world already knew his face. When he decided to go golfing with his dad in London that day, he had no idea that the craziest moment of his life was just hours away.

Holland's dad always wanted to be the star in the family. After grilling burgers for actors Ewan McGregor and Naomi Watts, he figured he was close enough.

Spider-Man has long been thought one of the best role models for kids. This is so true that a huge Spider-Man balloon is often part of parades all over the world.

Destined to Be Spider-Man

In many ways, Holland was destined to play Spider-Man. He started wearing Spider-Man costumes when he was little. He would stand in front of the mirror and strike poses. He would pretend to shoot webs from his wrists at bad guys. He taught himself to do flips and jumps, often scaring his dog, Tessa, when he knocked things over. Holland loved Spider-Man so much, he went to a party dressed as the superhero, even though no one else had dressed up.

He also had a best friend who loved Batman. They had endless debates of who would win in a fight: Batman or Spider-Man.

Now Holland takes every opportunity to go to his friend and tell him that he knows the answer. How? "Dude, I'm Spider-Man," Holland said in a Facebook interview filmed by Marvel.[1]

Holland auditioned to be Spider-Man many times over several months. Part of the audition process was reading lines with two Avengers: Captain America and Iron Man. Robert Downey Jr., who plays Iron Man, was impressed by Holland. He coached him during the filming of *Captain America: Civil War*.

Chris Hemsworth was another superhero who helped Holland. Without this actor, Holland might never have worn the Spider-Man costume onscreen. Hemsworth said in an interview with *The Daily News*, "I called the guys at Marvel when they were casting [Spider-Man] and I heard he was in the final handful of guys and said, 'Look, for what it's worth, you're not going to meet a harder working, more appreciative kind of guy.' " When asked why he was so impressed, Hemsworth added, "I was so blown away by his sort of attitude and work ethic and how he was, but then I said to Tom, 'I've told them that, so don't prove me wrong.' "[2]

There's a lot of training involved in becoming a superhero. For Holland, that included learning martial arts, gymnastics, CrossFit, and boxing. He also did something called EMS, or electronic muscle stimulation. Often used in therapy, EMS applies small electrical shocks to muscles. The therapy helped strengthen Tom's muscles while he exercised.

Holland didn't just train physically for the role. Because he had grown up in London, he had to learn to sound like a high school student in the United States. To do this, he went undercover. Marvel enrolled him in a New York high school.

After a few days, he couldn't stand to keep his secret anymore. He told two students that he was going to play Spider-Man. They didn't believe him, and because he didn't have any proof yet, there was no way to convince them!

Holland's parents were extremely supportive of his new role. Because he was still a minor, they had to go on set with him. Dominic Holland tweeted, "This morning I had 4 sons and now I have 3 sons and 1 spider."[3] They also enjoyed meeting other celebrities.

Was being in an Avengers movie everything Tom Holland had hoped it would be? Getting to throw Captain America's shield was awesome. Taking Spider-Man selfies on fire escapes was pretty cool. Other parts were not quite as much fun, such as the fight scene at the airport in *Civil War*. This scene was one of the biggest and most complicated fight scenes in Marvel history. There were huge amounts of people there, including cameramen, actors, and multiple stunt doubles. Not only was the airport crowded, but it

The **Captain America: Civil War** *premiere party in London was Tom Holland's first chance to meet his fans on the red carpet. He was a hit!*

was also very hot. The heat was so bad, the actors' makeup ran down their faces. The actor for the character Vision, Paul Bettany, actually fainted.

When the Avengers cast wasn't filming, they were often found at the house Marvel had rented for Holland. There, they swam and watched movies. They had so much fun, Holland took pictures of everyone in the house and posted them online. In two hours, the front yard was full of reporters. Minutes later, Holland's cell phone rang with a call from Marvel with a request not to do that again.

Spider-Man was actually only in about thirty minutes of *Civil War.* Luckily enough for Holland's fans, the new Spider-Man was given his own movie. *Spider-Man: Homecoming* was scheduled to be released in July 2017.

How did Holland keep busy when he was not filming? He was teaching kids in a children's hospital how to shoot Spidey webs!

After visiting the children at the hospital, Holland posted online that meeting them was "such a wonderful experience and you're all such little inspirations." [1]

Tom Holland enjoys playing Spider-Man, both onscreen and in real life. At the Henrietta Egleston Hospital for Children in Atlanta, Georgia, Holland taught sick kids how to stand like Spider-Man and how to pretend to shoot webs from their wrists. He let them take photos of him. He even allowed a boy with the superhero Deadpool on his T-shirt to take a video of him! If Holland's smile is anything to judge by, there weren't any hard feelings.

Whenever Holland isn't working or visiting kids in the hospital, he likes to visit his family. "When I come home, I'm still Tom," he said in an interview with *The Guardian*. "I still have to do the dishes and clean my room."[2]

Just as Peter Parker is a regular teen when he takes off his Spidey mask, Holland too is a normal guy when he's not in the Spider-Man costume. He watches his favorite movies, such as *Saving Private Ryan*. He listens to some of his favorite artists, including Ed Sheeran.

Holland enjoys posting on Instagram and Twitter. Whenever he practices his stunts or goes on hikes, he makes sure to post photos afterward. He also travels. When he was in Bangkok, Thailand, he ate a rat on a stick! He said, "It was disgusting. I'll never do it again. It was a mistake."[3]

When asked if he looks to the future and what his dream role would be, Holland's answer is easy. In ten years, he would love to play James Bond.

Holland is involved in a lot of films without his superhero suit. *The Current War* is about the race to harness electricity. It is full of other actors who have played in superhero movies. Benedict Cumberbatch (Doctor Strange) plays Thomas Edison, Nicholas Hoult (X-Men's Beast) plays Nikola Tesla, and Michael Shannon (*Man of Steel's* General Zod) plays George Westinghouse.

Holland plays younger Samuel Insull (left, front) who was the assistant to Thomas Edison (front, center) in the battle of inventor against inventor.

Tom Holland plays one of a group of monks in **Pilgrimage.** *Jon Bernthal says that audition tapes he and Holland created for Marvel still exist, but that getting to see them would be like "breaking into Fort Knox."*[4]

Meanwhile *Pilgrimage*, which was filmed in 2015, was scheduled for release in 2017. Holland plays a monk in the movie, alongside actor Jon Bernthal. During the film, the two actors helped each other prepare audition tapes for Marvel. Bernthal wanted the role of The Punisher in *Daredevil*, and Holland was still hoping to be the newest Spider-Man. Bernthal said in an interview with *The Daily News*, "We were making tapes from Ireland in the process of getting him cast in Spider-Man and then he and I made a tape for The Punisher."[5] Both, as we now know, were successful in landing their desired parts.

Holland's next film would be *Chaos Walking*, based on a young adult book by Patrick Ness. Due to be released in 2018, the film is about a world in which almost all the women have died. Holland's character meets the one

Spider-Man: Homecoming *will see Holland playing a 15-year-old Peter Parker* in high school. This means his costars will be much younger than in **Civil War**, *but if Holland's friendship with Zendaya Coleman (right) is anything to judge* *by, Holland doesn't mind too much.*

woman still alive. She is played by Daisy Ridley, the actor who plays Rey in *Star Wars: The Force Awakens.*

Fans might worry that *Spider-Man: Homecoming* will be the last time they will see Holland in his Spidey suit, but that is not true. The young actor has been contracted to star in a total of six future Marvel movies, including the next Avengers installment, *Infinity War.* The rest of Holland's future Marvel movies remain a mystery.

If your Spidey sense is tingling, it should be. It is telling you that you are going to be seeing Tom Holland sling webs across the screen for many years to come.

1996 Thomas Stanley Holland is born on June 1 in Kingston Upon Thames, England, UK.

2006 Tom performs at the Richmond Dance Festival with Nifty Feet Dance School.

2008 He performs in *Billy Elliot: The Musical.*

2010 He and three other actors who play Billy Elliot are invited to meet the prime minister of England.

2010 Holland provides the voice of Shô for Studio Ghibli's *The Secret World of Arrietty.*

2012 He enrolls in the BRIT School for Performing Arts and Technology.

2012 He stars in his first film, *The Impossible.*

2013 He is chosen as one of the first "Breakthrough Brits" by BAFTA (the British Academy of Film and Television Arts).

2015 He is chosen to play Spider-Man in *Captain America: Civil War.*

2017 Holland stars in *Spider-Man: Homecoming.*

FILMOGRAPHY

2018 *Chaos Walking* (Movie)

Avengers: Infinity War (Movie)

2017 *The Current War* (Movie)

Pilgrimage (Movie)

Spider-Man: Homecoming (Movie)

2016 *Captain America: Civil War* (Movie)

Edge of Winter (Movie)

The Lost City of Z (Movie)

2015 *Wolf Hall* (TV Series)

Tweet (Short)

In the Heart of the Sea (Movie)

2013 *Locke* (Movie)

How I Live Now (Movie)

2012 *The Impossible* (Movie)

2010 *The Secret World of Arrietty* (Voice)

Chapter 1

1. YouTube, *Tom Holland Spider-Man Homecoming Facebook Live Interview*, December 10, 2016. https://www.youtube.com/watch?v=1Cq2ZlAJhoQ

Chapter 2

1. Dana Matthews, "Breakout Star Tom Holland on His Film Debut *The Impossible*," *Teen Vogue*, January 22, 2013. http://www.teenvogue.com/story/tom-holland-the-impossible

Chapter 3

1. Nick Curtis, "Meet Tom Holland, the 16-Year-Old Star of *The Impossible*," *The Evening Standard*, December 20, 2012. http://www.standard.co.uk/lifestyle/london-life/meet-tom-holland-the-16-year-old-star-of-the-impossible-8427023.html

2. Sarah Long, "The New Spider-Man: 8 Things to Know About Tom Holland," *SheKnows*, June 23, 2015. http://www.sheknows.com/entertainment/articles/1087552/things-to-know-about-tom-holland-the-new-Spider-Man

3. "Meg Rosoff on *How I Live Now*," Film4, http://www.film4.com/special-features/interviews/meg-rosoff-on-how-i-live-now

4. Edward Douglas, "Tom Holland Sets Sail in the Heart of the Sea," *ComingSoon*, December 8, 2015. http://www.comingsoon.net/movies/features/638745-interview-tom-holland-sets-sail-in-the-heart-of-the-sea#/slide/1

Chapter 4

1. YouTube, *Tom Holland Spider-Man Homecoming Facebook Live Interview*, Facebook, December 10, 2016. https://www.youtube.com/watch?v=1Cq2ZlAJhoQ

2. Ethan Sacks, "Jon Bernthal and Tom Holland Made Audition Tapes Together to Land The Punisher and Spider-Man Roles," *New York Daily News*, March 10, 2016. http://www.nydailynews.com/entertainment/movies/exclusive-bernthal-holland-teamed-marvel-auditions-article-1.2560381

3. Rich Johnston, "Spider-Dad, Spider-Dad, Has Whatever a Spider-Dad Had," *Bleeding Cool*, June 24, 2015. https://www.bleedingcool.com/2015/06/24/spider-dad-spider-dad-has-whatever-a-spider-dad-had/

Chapter 5

1. Brian Gallagher, *Tom Holland Visits Children's Hospital in Spider-Man Costume. MovieWeb*, n.d. http://movieweb.com/spider-man-homecoming-tom-holland-childrens-hospital/

2. Jim Palmer, "Captain America—Civil War: South London Spider-Man Tom Holland's Career in Pictures," *The Guardian*, April 13, 2016. http://www.yourlocalguardian.co.uk/leisure/latest/14423656.Captain_America___Civil_War__south_London_Spider_Man_Tom_Holland_s_career_in_pictures/

3. YouTube, *Tom Holland Spider-Man Homecoming Facebook Live Interview*, Facebook, December 10, 2016. https://www.youtube.com/watch?v=1Cq2ZlAJhoQ

4. Ethan Sacks, "Jon Bernthal and Tom Holland Made Audition Tapes Together to Land The Punisher and Spider-Man Roles," *New York Daily News*, March 10, 2016. http://www.nydailynews.com/entertainment/movies/exclusive-bernthal-holland-teamed-marvel-auditions-article-1.2560381

5. Ibid.

Books

Sjoerdsma, Al, and Stuart Vandal. *Amazing Spider-Man: Official Index to the Marvel Universe.* New York: Marvel, 2010.

Spider-Man: Inside the World of Your Friendly Neighborhood Hero. New York: DK Children's Books, 2012.

Wallace, Daniel. *Spider-Man Character Encyclopedia.* New York: DK Children's Books, 2014.

Works Consulted

Eidell, Lynsey. "8 Things to Know About Tom Holland, the Super Cute New Spider-Man." *Glamour.* June 2015. http://www.glamour.com/story/tom-holland-new-spider-man-facts

Flessa, Maria-Elpida. "Tom Holland Trivia: 24 Facts You Didn't Know About the Actor!" *Useless Daily.* December 2016. http://www.uselessdaily.com/movies/tom-holland-trivia-24-facts-you-didnt-know-about-the-actor/#.WIZ0kIgrLnA

Kenny, Lucy. "11 Reasons You'll Be Obsessed with New Spider-Man Tom Holland." *Pop Sugar.* June 2016. https://www.popsugar.co.uk/celebrity/British-Actor-Tom-Holland-Facts-41203742#photo-41203742

Longeretta, Emily. "Tom Holland: 5 Things to Know About the New Spider-Man." *Hollywood Life.* June 2015. http://hollywoodlife.com/2015/06/23/tom-holland-bio-spider-man-facts/

Mahajan, Mradula. "12 Facts to Know About New Spider-Man: Tom Holland." *Movie News Guide.* June 2015. http://www.movienewsguide.com/12-facts-to-know-about-new-spider-man-tom-holland/71003

Mitchell, Maurice. "10 Interesting Facts You Need to Know About Tom Holland." *The Geek Twins.* June 2015. http://www.thegeektwins.com/2015/06/10-interesting-facts-you-need-to-know.html#.WIZzuYgrLnA

Perez, Angela. "Tom Holland Is Best Spider-Man Ever? 8 Amazing Facts About Him." *Aussie Network News.* March 2016. http://www.australianetworknews.com/tom-holland-best-spider-man-ever-8-amazing-facts/

Reading, Caleb. "Here's How Tom Holland Nailed His Audition for Spider-Man." *UPROXX.* May 2016. http://uproxx.com/gammasquad/tom-holland-spider-man-audition/

On the Internet

Instagram: Tom Holland
https://www.instagram.com/tomholland2013/?hl=en

Internet Movie Database: Tom Holland
http://www.imdb.com/name/nm4043618/

Marvel
http://marvel.com

GLOSSARY

animate (AN-ih-may-te)—To bring drawings to life on film.

audition (aw-DIH-shun)—To try out for a part in a movie or play.

comedian (kuh-MEE-dee-in)—A person who tells funny stories on stage.

free running (FREE RUN-ing)—A sport in which a person jumps and leaps over things for fun.

stimulation (stim-yoo-LAY-shun)—Making active or more active.

stunt double (STUNT DUH-bul)—A person who does the dangerous moves in movies instead of actors.

trampoline (TRAMP-puh-leen)—A stretchy sheet supported by springs and a frame on which people can bounce and tumble.

tsunami (tsoo-NAH-mee)—A very large wave of water, usually caused by an earthquake under the ocean.

INDEX